Tommy's Afraid to Try

Created and illustrated by
Joanne (Jodie) McCallum

Written by
Barbara Linville

©1989 Merchandising Development Corp.
in cooperation with McCallum Design Co.
Published by The STANDARD PUBLISHING Company, Cincinnati, Ohio.
Division of STANDEX INTERNATIONAL Corporation. Printed in U.S.A.
Library of Congress Catalog Card Number 89-062628

"Hi ya, Higher Ark," said Angel Encourage as she ran into Higher Ark's office. With one leap of her bunny feet, she landed smack on Higher Ark's desk and sat there, looking up at him, her long white ears tickling his chin. "You wanted to see me?" she asked.

Higher Ark brushed the tickly ears away and sneezed. "Can't you ever just sit on a chair like other angels?" he complained.

"Sure, Higher Ark," replied Angel Encourage, hopping down. "If it'll make you happy." Then over to the chair she went, climbing up into it and letting her feet kick back and forth as she sat there.

Higher Ark sighed and said, "Sometimes, Angel Encourage, I wonder about you." Then he smiled and added, "But I think you're just the one to help little Tommy Taylor down there on earth."

"How?" asked Encourage. "What's wrong with poor old Tom."

"Poor old Tom," Higher Ark began. Then he shut his eyes and shook his head. "I mean, little Tommy, is afraid. He won't play baseball or answer questions in school or even try new things to eat. He is absolutely terrified of trying."

The white bunny's eyebrows rose up in surprise. "Well, I'd better be on my way to earth then," she said, sliding down from her chair. "Just bring on the down-cloud and we'll get this show on the road."

Higher Ark stared down at Encourage with a gaping mouth.

"What's the matter, Higher Ark?" Encourage asked. "Don't you want me to go to earth and help Tommy Taylor learn to try?"

"Yes, I want you to go to earth and help Tommy Taylor learn to try," Higher Ark replied grumpily. "I would just like a chance to say so, that's all."

"Well, go ahead," said Encourage. "I'll listen."

Higher Ark looked up at the ceiling and sighed and said, "Oh, never mind." Then he snapped his fingers for the down-cloud and it came and settled on the floor at Encourage's feet. In a moment she had bounced onto the little cloud, and Higher Ark was sprinkling halo dust over her and saying,

Down to earth now you descend
To help our little "won't-try" friend.

Then down, down, down, Encourage shot. Right down through the stars and past the moon and under the clouds. Right down to Tommy's house and into Tommy's backyard. And as soon as Angel Encourage's foot touched the grass, she became a little soft and cuddly toy bunny. Bump, roll, bump, bump, roll— Encourage spun over the grass and came to rest at the bottom of a fence.

And there, looking over the fence, was Tommy. He was watching a ball game in the empty lot across the street and looking very lonely.

"Hey, Tom!" called out Encourage. "Why don't you go over there and play with those kids? They're having fun. Oh, and by the way, my name is Encourage. Nice to meet ya."

Tommy bent down to look at the toy bunny lying on the ground. Then he picked it up and held it close. "Hi, Encourage," he said. "Will you be my friend?"

"Sure, sure," Encourage replied. "Just watch it that you don't hug the stuffings out of me, that's all."

Tommy loosened his hold a bit.

"Yeah, that's better," panted Encourage. When she got her breath back, she said, "Now look here, Tom. It's time you went across the street and joined in the game. Enough of standing here."

Tommy just hung his head. "But all the other kids are bigger than I am," he said. "I can't do what they do."

"Horsefeathers!" replied Encourage. "How can you know until you try? You've got feet for running and hands for catching and eyes for seeing just the same as they've got."

"But they know what to do," Tommy said, "and I don't."

One of Encourage's ears drooped down over her eye. "So we'll go over and watch for awhile first. How's that?" she asked brightly.

"Okay," said Tommy. "I'll ask my mom if I can go. But I'm not going to play or anything." Then he hurried to ask his mother if he could go across the street and watch the game.

"Of course, Tommy," she said. "But be back by dinnertime. We're having broccoli souffle tonight."

"Broccoli souffle," muttered Tommy as he walked away. "I wonder what that is. Probably something awful."

It was still early spring and the days were still a bit blustery and cool, so Tommy had on his jacket with the big pockets in it. And now he placed the toy bunny in one of those pockets so that just her head and ears stuck out.

"Nice goin', Tom," Encourage said. "I can ride in here just fine and still see everything."

So Tommy and Encourage went across the street and sat down on an old tree stump and watched the other children playing ball. One big boy came up to home plate, lifted the bat and stood crouching, waiting for the ball to come.

"Look at that guy, Tom," Encourage whispered. "See how he's holding the bat? See how he stands? You could do that, Tom. I know you could."

"I don't know," said Tommy doubtfully.

Just then, whack! The boy hit the ball far out into the field and then ran for first base and then for second and stopped.

Encourage cheered and whistled between her two big front teeth. "Wooeee, Tom!" she said then. "Doesn't that make you want to get out there and slug that old ball into the outfield?"

"Sort of," Tommy admitted. "But I don't think I could."

"Oh, but you could, you could, Tommy."

Encourage's words rang out so cheerfully and clear that for a moment, Tommy almost thought he could try, but then he shook his head. He was still too afraid.

But Encourage was not ready to give up. "Okay, Tom, okay," she said. "Let's watch this next batter and see what happens."

The next batter was a girl not much bigger than Tommy. She hit the ball into left field and dashed for first base, her long braids flying out behind her.

Again Encourage yelled and whistled. Then she spoke softly to Tommy. "Hey, Tom," she said as though she had a secret. "I just noticed something. Count the number of players out there on the field and tell me how many you see."

Tommy counted carefully, then answered, "Eight."

"You're right, Tom," Encourage replied. "That's not enough. They need one more player. Why don't you ask to play, Tom? You could do it. I know you could."

"I wish I could," Tommy said in a wistful voice. "Do you really think I can play?"

"I think you can try," replied Encourage. "First you gotta try. And then you gotta try some more. And if you try long enough and hard enough you'll finally know if you can play or not. What do you say, Tom? Want to give it a try?"

Tommy looked out at the players on the field again and then said, "Maybe."

"Attaboy, Tom!" exclaimed Encourage. "I knew you would."

So when the teams changed sides, Tommy asked if he could play. The leader of the team said he could and stuck him at the end of the long line of batters. That was okay with Tommy who still felt a little afraid of going up to bat.

But only two of the players made outs. And the rest either scored points or got on base. Then all of a sudden Tommy was next! Swallowing hard, he walked up to home plate and picked up the bat.

"Attaboy, Tom," whispered Encourage from Tommy's pocket. "Remember how you hold the bat, how you stand. That's it. That's it. Get ready now. That old ball's going to be whizzing down here any minute and ..."

Whiz! The ball had gone by and Tommy had not even swung the bat! "I knew it," he said mournfully. "This is even worse than I thought it would be."

"Don't worry about it, Tom," Encourage reassured him. "Talk to God about it. That's a great helper-outer. Now get ready for the next pitch. Think, Tom, think."

Whiz! The ball hurtled toward home plate again. This time Tommy did manage to swing the bat, though the ball was nowhere near it at the time. "Missed again," Tommy said in disappointment. "I knew it. I'm just no good at anything."

"Wait! Don't say that yet," Encourage told him. "So you missed the ball. You'll see it better next time and you'll know when to swing the bat."

Tommy was watching the pitcher's every move now. He saw the ball leave his hand. He saw the ball coming, coming. Tommy swung. Plok! He hit the ball. But the ball did not fly straight into outfield as Tommy hoped it would. Instead it flew up, right in front of his nose, and came down near his foot. Then it started rolling down toward third base. He had failed again.

But, suddenly, Encourage yelled out, "It's good, Tommy. RUN!"

Tommy dropped the bat and raced toward first base.

"Attaboy, Tom," the little white rabbit in Tommy's pocket went on yelling. "Faster, Tom, faster!"

Tommy's short legs churned down toward first base so fast that he fell and slid the rest of the way. But when the dust cleared away, his hand was on the base and he was safe.

Encourage was trying to yell and whistle and laugh all at once, but the dust from Tommy's slide was still in her nose and eyes. "Mimfl rumfl, ha ha, ah-choo!" was all she could say.

But Tommy's teammates were cheering too. "Hooray, for Tommy!" they shouted.

And Tommy stood at first base, cheering as well.

"I knew it, Tom," Encourage was able to say at last. "I knew you could do it."

"It really wasn't a very good hit," Tommy replied.

Encourage only laughed. "But it *was* a hit, Tom. Remember, ya gotta try, and then ya gotta try some more, before you can get good at anything. Well, you did try. And you're starting to get good! Hooray, Tom!"

And then Angel Encourage sent her thoughts up to Higher Ark. "Well, Higher Ark, mission accomplished. Tommy's beginning to try. But hang around for my next message. 'Cause next, Tommy and I are going to tackle broccoli souffle. Goodbye for now, Higher Ark."